I0756249

FINISHING LINE PRESS
www.finishinglinepress.com

Body of Work

poems by

Rowe Carenen

Finishing Line Press
Georgetown, Kentucky

Body of Work

For Fred, Hannah, Molly, and the Bean
and
for Christine: Thank you for coming over to tell me you liked my hair and inviting me to sushi

ISBN 979-8-89990-401-1 First Edition

ACKNOWLEDGMENTS

"Sick," "Sick Enough," and "Enough" all appeared in the digital version of *Womanly Mag*'s Fat issue
"Ethel" appeared in the 8th issue of *Oyster River Pages*

Publisher: Leah Huete de Maines
Editor: Christen Kincaid
Cover Art: *Balasana* by Sunny Mullarkey, 2014. Oil on canvas, 12"x16
Author Photo: James Huffman
Cover Design: Elizabeth Maines McCleavy

Order online: www.finishinglinepress.com
also available on amazon.com

Author inquiries and mail orders:
Finishing Line Press
PO Box 1626
Georgetown, Kentucky 40324
USA

Contents

Where Do I Go

I don't know who told me first
to be small, to be little, to shrink
down to less than in order
to fit.

I have starved on honey-
dew and stewed cabbage,
savoring a blueberry NutriGrain
bar over three days
only to lose not enough.

I think I was 11 when
I noticed my belly rolls
were no longer cute, but
by the time they were gone
my breasts had arrived.

Some disease or other
whittled away my waist
and my cheekbones knife-
edged their way to prominence.
My then-husband squeezed my
jutting hips and said he was proud.

Today I snuck rosemary shortbread
from my favorite bookstore, a pre-meeting
treat and the guilt was stronger
than either the butter or the herb.

I have been all the sizes, all the weights,
and I don't know where
my body should live. They say
I am not my body, but how
else do you see me when we
sit down over a pinot and laugh
over cheats and praise when we are "good."

I don't know how not to think
about food/fat/rolls/dress size.
Sometimes I miss my collarbones

and sometimes they bruise from
protruding past the scarves
I hide behind.

Painted Toes

I have claimed victory
my fingernails are
passion red, a wintery
maroon without a bubble
or crack or chip. And I did
it my own self.

I'm nearly 42 and this
is my pandemic accomplishment,
no baking or new language
or a knitted home
for surplus toilet paper.

But my toes are a miasma
of Rorschach splotches,
uneven, cracked, depressingly
naked.

I lamented my failure
to Evelyn while she watched
Canadian snow out her window
and I prayed for a Thanksgiving
that allowed sweaters and not sweat.

She laughed, at me, as usual, and
told me she'd never met anyone
who could pedicure their
ownselves successfully.

And that's just it—
the revelation—I am not
alone in my failure. It is a myth
like folding fitted sheets. Or
day to night fashion
and work/life balance.

I don't understand

time anymore, although
I'm not sure I ever did.

I don't know when
it stopped being February
but yesterday was 90 degrees
and Neville dug under the bushes
because there is no AC outside.

The hygienist asked about the ring
that is not THE ring, just A ring, and
I couldn't help but talk of you. She asked
how long and I said just over a year.

But that can't be right—we have known
one another through disease/death/divorce;
decades don't seem long enough
and yet the calendar says not quite
twenty years since we met.

So I'll just say forever.
I've known you forever
and will know you forever
and still that's not long enough.

I don't understand time.

This is not the poem I intended

We are not young
and our decades-long orbit
wove around seas and continents,
pirates, blizzards, hurricanes,
silence.

We have circled and come back
to all-in couch cuddles on Sunday
mornings with Carolands milk clouds
in coffee and tea steeped just right.

I fought, you fought,
to say love and hold hands
while strolling through Publix
to decide apples or pears
in tonight's salad.

I spiraled through my unstable
planet, started at the crust
of an ever-expanding
body that shifts and softens
with disappearing clavicles
and hip bones, into the mantle
of a malleable credit score and an
inability to build modular furniture,
next the magnetism of unpublished
poems and barren uterus vie in the liquid
outer core, finally hitting the inner core
that feels cracked through
with every failure birthed that could
not leave the iron graveyard.

You listened, leaning against the crumb-
covered counters in the kitchen
while my wailing quieted into
hodge-podge breaths. And said
let's build the couch together,
beautiful. You showed me the error
was yours, that of course I couldn't
do it alone. It would have to take two.

When I started this,
I wanted to write
of Scottish scarves
and painted stars
and perfect proposals
between fantasy and
romance, but I've changed
my mind. I want
to live in the words
and spaces hard-won.

You know the truth of me
and made your choice,
so here we are—
for better and worse.

Nocturnal Wringing

I don't know when I started
to hold my own hands,
stashed under navy satin
pillowcases that are supposed to
prevent more wrinkles
on my already lined face,

while I sleep, not gripped
like a proper British choir—
fingertips to knuckles, a strong
hold not to come undone—
but my right hand over the left,
squeezing tight.

When I wake, stretching
and uncurling before dawn,
hefting the asylum grey
weighted blanked off
my still weary body,
sometimes
there's an ache in the bones.

Sick

The cost of not eating
enough is freedom.

I have chained myself
to plans/programs/apps
all promising to teach
what it means to be
full, satisfied, enough.

Like a con looking to beat
the systems, underestimating
the elliptical hours
overestimating the cupcake
calories, spitting the buttercream
into the can under my desk
hiding it under last month's P&L report,
offering to take out the trash,
to throw away
my shame.

Sauté is a swear and oil the sin.
I sing the merits
of bouillon and an air fryer.
Afraid of the sodium in my favorite
pickles, I drink gallons
of celery juice to wash away the salt.
I've forgotten the texture
of spaghetti; having built
my cell of mushroom noodles
that squeak with each bite.

Once after a yoga class,
I told my teacher how much I ran,
that I loved the sound of sneakers
on sidewalks, but
sometimes my knees/hips/back
ached. She suggested I walk
instead, and I said it's not
the same. "Ah, so what
are you running from?"

Me. I'm running from me.

Picky Hippy

I have loved matcha tea
in all its grassy glory
for decades. I'm not a purist
nor do I honor the ceremonial
whisk and bowl. I'm happy with drive-
thru, iced or hot with almond
or oat milk. At home I use a double
coiled frother to blend jade
powder for drinking, accepting
there will be mug mud, adding
extra water to make up the difference.
I've even jumped on the strawberry
trend and my tea comes in the shape
of Hello Kitty and makes me giggle
every single time I drop it into the hand
hewn mug. I take a picture
and send it to Natasha who is still
holding a grudge that I did not
bring her a coin purse from a New York
street vendor in 2013.

I delight in a delicate summertime
cucumber sandwich, sliced thin:
schmear of mayo, a kiss
of dill on white bread
cut on the diagonal
with all crusts removed.
James gives me his pickles;
I love them and he loves
my happy dance when he plops
the salty spear on the side of my
Styrofoam takeout box.

But on our standing Wednesday lunch
date at the new Mediterranean build-
your-own-bowl joint, Christine and I discovered
cucumber water is a monstrosity
and I will not subject my taste buds
to a crime against flavor. The pulpy
yard clippings clogging my paper
straw is just wrong; a blended

disappointing and sad smoothie
that gets my ire up so high
I'm willing to go to the mattresses in a white
chocolate is not chocolate attack.

So much of the world is on fire
and I both light the truth torches
and bring water to douse the lies
but the inconsequential is today's hill.

Midterms

I went to the doctor this week
to see about the swelling (ankle,
foot, lymph nodes), I have
insurance now and I don't have
to worry about giving up the fancy
fizzy waters to pay the bill.

I'm fine, probably. Age
and allergies. No blood clots
and not cancer. Probably.

But my throat still feels full
up of all I don't say,
hoarse from screaming existence
into silence; yelling back at the Proud
Boy mocking my "vote" shirt
seems like a poor choice. I order
a medicine ball, the soothing honey
only helps so much.

There is irony that this week
I'm ovulating, my body preparing
to conceive a life it would
destroy and I don't know
if I have the words to adequately
articulate the grief and the terror
and the anger and the despair.

So I smoke cleanse my house
with lavender and rosemary,
whispering over and over
"be a refuge, be a refuge..."

And I pray. Even more. Real
words to my God on my knees
that are bloody in supplication.

Permanent

Slipping out of my cozy
work from home stretch pants
into stiff jeans to meet Christine
for her birthday lunch, purple squigglies
catch my eye. They run from just below
my belly button down to the fold above
my incision from the latest surgery.

At seventeen, my disease discovered
because some young doctor thought
my appendix was about to rupture, lasered
off what he could find of the endometrial
growths, removing the appy was a bonus.
Birth control script and I'd be fine.

At 20 the pain came back so surgery
was on the docket, but first menopause.
The expert surgeon slipped in
hysterectomy as an option for the cutting
scheduled the day after I turned 21.
Turns out my organs were saved,
but I'd never conceive/carry/deliver.

At 43 I learned it isn't the disease, but
the treatment, that stole motherhood
from me. I'm trying, sometimes daily,
to give those doctors grace, to remember
they did the best they could
with what they knew. At least I got to skip
the electrodes to my head to treat
the hysteria of my "hostile uterus".

Six and a half weeks ago, I had my insides
scraped again, third time's a charm,
to see if this time the new doc could stop
the ten-day hemorrhaging of clots, maybe
minimize the fireworks and fists
of cramps that don't just dance through
my abdomen and back, but skate down my thighs.

These stretchmarks, usually the result
of a bundle of joy, not a tangle of scars,
lesions, and a polyp, are a new kind
of malicious reminder, a permanent marker
that all I grow is destruction and discontent.

Sick Enough

The reward for not eating
enough is worthiness.

I've had decades of practice
faking full, bowls of bone
broth enough to fool my belly.
I study menus, finding
safe foods; fearfully scarf
whole spreads at parties; eat
only green beans and berries
the next week. I lie.

I zip up jeans in a size I haven't
worn since eighth grade, pinching
my side and untucking my "always be
brusselin'" tee; hide the bruises or blame
the dog; water pools in my clavicles.

I knew at six sloth is a sin
and fat a sign, a failure
of will and discipline, so I skip breakfast
for nine years, daily drink 180 ounces,
squat/lunge until my knees click and swell,
a not-yet suitable temple.

I told my therapist no
when she asked if I thought
I might have a problem
with food/eating/exercise.
I laughed. I eat every day
and this headache is just always
there and weightlifting and yoga
are hard and work is stressful
so I'm tired and everyone watches
what they eat and I don't keep bread in the house

and cauliflower is a better rice
and just because I've killed my appetite
and haven't had a hunger cue in years…

I don't look sick, so I must
be fine. I'm fine.

I'm fine I'm fine I'm fine.

Ethel

Ethel tells jokes so bad, she
adds "get it?" before slapping
her knee and wiping
the joy dripping off her face.

Ethel has scars criss-crossing her
legs from exploring the woods
with Charlotte the mastiff, reading "Little House"
on the u-shaped branch of her favorite tree.

Ethel makes world-class oatmeal raisin
cookies for all her friends, but only
in the fall when the air is crisp enough
for the cinnamon, nutmeg, clove.

While the tech rambles about strawberries
at Whole Foods, I squint between my stirrup-ed
feet at the ultrasound screen. The grey rabbit's foot
on the edge of my uterus was not Ethel.

When the surgeon lasers my insides
free of adhesions and scar tissue, she
will remove the only thing my body
is fit to grow, a polyp we've named Francis.

And I'll go home in post-partum panties
with painkillers and heating pads, curl
around the pregnancy pillow and pray this
time, this treatment, this surgery will work.

If I could've had a daughter,
I would've named her Ethel.

Seconds

This morning over savory waffles
and Gilmore Girls-themed lattes,
Christine asks how I'm feeling
about the wedding and it being my second.

I tell her I don't think of it as second,
I think of it as ours. She says it feels
like a first because we both forget sometimes
there was ever a before time.

I tell her loving him is the easiest
thing I've ever done in my life, easier
than breathing because sometimes
I forget to breathe, and I have to remember
to inhale AND exhale, but I never forget
to love him.

I tell her that I used to think
I was bad at being a wife, at loving,
and that it was just better for me to collect
cats and scarves and mugs and Care Bear
share my heart from a safe distance.

But safe isn't distance;
it's him, it's us.

It's always standing
in front of the drawer that holds
the potato masher and instead
of an eye-roll or sigh, it's a laughed
"of course" and butt smack.

It's watching the Barbie movie
and downloading Red (Taylor's
Version) for a fourteen-hour drive
across six states to meet the rest
of his family, and when I
was overwhelmed by doilies
and ornamental hatchets, sending
me to bed with a book so I could

decompress. It's the debrief
on the way home.

It's boozy tea on a Sunday morning
made for me while I snuggle in,
steeped just long enough
the bitterness is a memory.

Enough

The problem with not eating
enough is silence.

She was so casual in her switch
from disordered eating
to eating disorder. She didn't
even take a beat, a breath,
a momentary pause so I could…
respond? object? explain?

"That's your eating disorder talking,
not you," when I said
bread was a treat and rice was rare
and I allow one single dark chocolate
covered caramel with sea salt
a night. An indulgence that meant
I was fine. A serving size is three.

I was proud of my control
my discipline my willpower
to only eat one chocolate a night.
"But what if you wanted two?"
No, only one. And sometimes
not even that. "Ah, so the anorexia
is in charge."

Now at least three times a day
there's a starch/produce/protein/fat
and twice a combo of two. Every day
I hear whispers surfing the wrinkles
of my brain: I don't really need that
potato and an apple has too much sugar
and two bites is a serving, and you can say
you had a heavy lunch (your smoothie cup
is thick plastic so it isn't exactly a lie), you
skipped your workout instead of pushing
through the pain so you don't deserve breakfast,
but you can add some honey to your tea, but not
too much because you have to fit into your
wedding dress and you don't want
to be an embarrassment.

Enough. I say enough.

One Beautiful and Perfect Ovary

In college, I would spend hours
window-shopping Gap's online maternity
offerings: classic blue-striped dresses
with empire waists, clean khakis
with grow bands, crisp white button-ups
covered in cabled cardigans, simple silver
hoops peeking out from a perfectly
highlighted blonde bob, dreaming of how
classy I'd be pregnant.

I designed a Narnia-
themed nursery of hand-painted snowy
trees, a lamppost, and a faun
with an umbrella and presents bundled
under his arm, a wardrobe crammed with onesies
and soft, plushy blankets.

I'd stuff pillows under
the sweaters I stole from Dad every visit home,
supporting my back and easing into chairs.
I practiced breathing.

I didn't know yet that it wasn't just the disease
but the remedy, the burning away of tissue clusters
adhered to my uterus, ovaries, tubes, bladder, intestines,
that would steal the smell of my newborn's head, or that
John Gerald
Helen Elisabeth
Ethel Jane
would only be ephemeral whisps,
strangers that never were.

Today was my first Mother's Day without my uterus
and I'm supposed to be grateful for never having
babies with my older ex-husband who
cursed me for denying him a legacy, or for the end
of periods I've been used to powering through, or the lack
of shooting pain down my thighs and up my back
as fiery vices pinch my abdomen, or even for the abundance
of friends who brought meals and plush puppy heating pads, or

one beautiful and perfect ovary, and an actual partner who bought
a silver bell so that I wouldn't have to
raise my voice when I needed help
getting to the bathroom.

And I am, really I am, but

the anesthesiologist asked how I was
feeling other than my "girl problems"
and I'm still so mad I stutter in the telling;

I can't pick up my cat because the shelf they
built hasn't healed yet and my intestines
could come out of my vagina, or pour booze
into my decaf Earl Grey because the Carolands
bottle is too heavy and the strain leaves me
breathing hard, or sneeze without bracing
my arms against my stomach out of fear
I'll tear the sutures, or wash my hair
without resting my elbows on my breasts
and needing a nap before the shampoo
is even down the drain, or wear jeans
because I'm still too swollen and the fabric
is too stiff and because my digestive
organs are sloshing and thunking like an alien
I can sometimes see pressing against my skin
settling into the newly empty space,

I can't sweep the pollen
and jasmine blossoms off the porch because
it might lead to emergency reconstructive surgery,
sit in my pumpkin chair because getting in and out
engages my core too much, sleep through the night
because I rolled over funny and it feels like
a ringlet curling iron is dancing in my insides,
do yoga because even child's pose causes more
bleeding and I'm so damn tired of the blood.

Yesterday I cut my own toenails and cried.

In sickness and in health

I grew up knowing what love looked like,
had it modeled in burned-out flipped
electric blankets and birthday hamloaf,
hands held in church and butts pinched
in kitchens when I wasn't supposed to see.

But the ex told me what I believed marriage
to be was a fantasy sold by Disney and Hollywood
and that's why Jane Austen's books stopped
at the wedding. He was wrong, but I was scared.

Less than two months after our vows, my now
husband knew my throat would be sore from
the tube helping me breathe when my favorite
surgeon sliced out five of my mothering organs,
so he ordered a silver bell for me to ring.

The morning after, I couldn't get out of bed, so
he helped move my legs, set my feet on the ground,
put my hands on his shoulders, his on my back. I tried
to be steady, to inhale deep for strength, but the shakes
wouldn't stop and my voice cracked, "I can do this
I can do this I can do this."

He let loose tears because I couldn't,
helped me to the couch, made me a boozy tea,
and queued up Bridgerton.

He told me I was beautiful in my maternity
panties and high-waisted 3X sanitarium grey
sweatpants, unfolded the shower wipes and helped
me clean the hospital off, washed my hair in the sink
because I couldn't stand the feeling of gunk sticking
to my neck, my forehead.

He nuked the lavender heating
pad puppy and tucked it up against the wedge
pillow that made me sleep upright.

He set reminders on his phone
to make sure I kept up the cocktail
of pills to keep the pain and infection away, slept
on the couch for days, afraid he'd rollover to cuddle
and cause pain.

He snuggled the critters and
tried to sing Tia her song
because I couldn't.

I told him once that I hate Jake Gyllenhaal
and Adam Levine and when I told him why
he said, "ok then, we hate them. We
hate together, baby." And so we do.

He holds a grudge because a book
I recommended broke his heart and will never
go back to the brewery for being unkind to the son of
our friend and loves my mother's fig bars and gave her
hard labor for Christmas.

He loaned my best friend Alice the Jeep
so her son could ride out fifth grade in style.

He found the complete Anne of Green Gables
DVDs for me and bought my tickets
to the island in October.

And now cancer. Another surgery. Another organ
ousted, another recovery.

And I know what love looks like.

A Conversation with Hope

I sent Hope to her room.
It is not safe here for songs
of encouragement and lyrics of, "77%
is only 3/4ths! Ish. It will be fine."

Because it won't be.

I tell her how much I love her
how we've shored each other
up for ages now and I know we
always come out ok and the darkness
passes and fall is joyous and bright leaves
slip into muted jewels and tea is better
on the porch when the air is crisp
and we've gotten through everything else.

But it isn't safe for her right now
because the anger is strangling me
and I can't catch my breath and sometimes
swallowing is too hard and I feel full up
with words that can't get beyond this
lump in my throat. Three surgeries
thirteen months, six organs
exiled.

And just this once when the doctor said we
ought to check this out, I believed
all would be well. Just this once
it didn't register that it wouldn't. Just
this one time I got the ticket to Canada,
purchased the luggage and planned the sweaters,
and told everyone not to worry—
there's no way it could be
cancer.

I held hands with Hope.

But now I need her to go
away until I'm ready to sing
the songs and weave forget-me-nots
into her braid and believe
again.

Daffodils

I was talking to Evelyn on Monday,
well not *talking*, leaving a voice memo
as is my practice most days while walking
my morning loops in the tea-stained
hoodie Mom gave me for Christmas
four years ago, telling her how my stomach
tightens and nausea roils up my throat,
my hands keep forming fists so tight
I have crescents in my palms over our
country, well mine; she's now Canadian.

Two men, during an Idaho town hall
Saturday, hauled a woman out in zip
ties because she dared to speak loudly.
She disagreed with the moderator and
said so. The men who refused to identify
themselves, put their hands on her body,
shoved her to the ground, restrained her.
"This little girl does not want to leave.
She spoke up and now does not want
to suffer the consequences."
She was charged with assault. I see her
lost shoe in the aisle when I close my eyes.
Her cries to not touch her ricochet in my brain.

Measles are back in Texas and Georgia,
children are dying. My friend in bio
medical investigation warned of the next
epidemic, death tolls in unimaginable
numbers decades of research wiped.
She's been censured, her lab an echoed
warning as colleagues file for unemployment.
My sister tells me her friends in cancer
research are rowing directionless
in the same boat and I think of Christine
whose tumors are shrinking, but we know
the growths could tiptoe back to her brain,
her lungs, and her oncologist's hope
was in some trial or new med.

Saturday, we took a mixed dozen macarons
pink and green and yellow circles of sweetness
lined up like individual promises in the long
box, and a handful of giant heart-shaped sugar
cookies iced in the pastels of Spring to the Travelers
Rest library. The librarians had to remove
their Black History Month and Women in STEM
displays amid promises to end their lives
or "*just fuck the wokeness away.*" All I could
do was thank them for choosing to stay
and be a free space for all people.
And *they* thanked *me*.

There's just so much shit,
there are daffodils in my yard.

Because I Can

I was listening to Anne Lamont
on NPR while I logged miles
in my driveway. She told
the story of shopping with her friend
(who was dying of cancer)
for a new dress to impress Anne's latest
boyfriend. The friend said she didn't
have the time to worry if the dress
made Anne's thighs look wide.

I thought about why I do these miles,
why I do the squats and the planks,
the triceps kickbacks. Lifting heavy
things and putting them down again
and again and again. It used to be
because my ex-husband was never satisfied
with my body, with me. Before that, the
pastor's son left me for cheerleaders.

Somewhere in the last 45 years,
I learned to shape my body
to make other people proud,
to be seen with me
to be known by me.

But then five organs were ripped
from my abdomen through tiny
little holes, and the scars and growths
were burned off with lasers.
Stitches disappeared into wrinkles
and folds of my never-pregnant belly,
swollen to third-trimester girth.

Now, on Thursday, another organ
will be sliced from my throat,
and my voice will be paused
if not silenced, and I had to buy
new jammies with a breast pocket
to hold the drain so my arms won't
fatigue under the weight of all I lost,
am losing.

And I walk my miles. Every day. Small
loops with pauses to scratch the heads
of the Ferals and tell Neville he's a good boy.
Soon I won't be able to complete this tour
of concrete and dying grass. And when I can,
the pauses will be longer, the recovery months.

But today I get the circuit in. Because I can.
Because I need the strength to carry me
through. I'm not yet eight months married
and the new husband glories in me
and my body, and I need it to be whole
for me, and for him, and
because my parents are not young
and I want to help my mother
rearrange the living room, again, just to put it
back the way it was.
Because the Iowa Hawkeyes
need to get it together and
I want to watch the games
with Dad and comment on how I can't believe they're
running that play again because everyone knows they're
going to run that play again.
Because my goddaughters are thirteen and seven,
and I want to show them strength and softness
and that love is not what your body looks like or what it can do.

And so I walk and lift the weights and put them down
and hold the stretches.
Until the discomfort lessons.
Because I can.

Someone is outside playing saxophone

while I drink once hot tea and try not
to focus on my best friend's cancer.

It was supposed to be me.

I know how to be sick and
I know how to fight and
it was supposed to be me.

But I don't have cancer;
just a necrotic thyroid, gone now,
and I take tiny pills every morning
to keep me fine.

This multiplying menace will steal
her curves and her hair and her energy
and she's worried because the bathrooms
are too far from the bedrooms in her house.

We can do this.

I can help her donate her hair
sit during chemo
organize meals and flowers
go to all of the kids' shows
decorate for Christmas
crack jokes and pick out wigs
offer books and blankets so soft
that her skin can stand the touch.

But I cannot take this from her.
I cannot save her children from
watching their mother wither.
I cannot save her from seeing
the fear in their faces as they cuddle
as close as she can bear.

I do believe she will beat this.
I do believe she will endure.

But what I would do to save her from this.
To save us all.

Strong Soft Safe

On December 26th I texted Christine
to see how her Christmas hangover
was progressing (too many people,
too many presents, too much food,
and chemo the next day). She asked
if she could please come over and just
sit on my couch for a while. Of course.
The answer is always of course.

I waited, unwashed and wearing
the same cozies from the whole week
before, scrolled through Instagram
and learned I was doing it wrong.
Finish the year strong! Crush
those goals! Jumpstart your
resolutions! Start now! Push! Push!
PUSH! Or, Take naps! Bake bread!
Buy cashmere pants! Your knees
will love them!

But as Christine came in (equally
unwashed and comfy), unpacked
takeout curry on the coffee table,
and we folded ourselves into our
claimed corners, I realized I only
wanted to end the year safe.

I yearn for you to feel the comfort
of a twenty-year friendship, the joy
of the perfect curry to rice ratio, the
unwavering hope that this time Mom
will let the good boy sleep in the bed.

With Thanks

First, huge thanks to Christen and Mimi, and everyone else at Finishing Line Press. They have been a dream, and I can't think of a better home for this collection.

Caroline and Lauren of Gold Leaf Literary have been exceedingly helpful in getting this introvert out of her comfort zone of quietly drinking tea and reading books to herself and poems to her friends out into the world. Without you, I would sit in my cozy chair and wish I had shared these words with more readers.

Thank you to Sunny Malarkey McGowan, my friend and incredible artist, for letting me use her breathtaking piece as my cover art. You inspire me and comfort me all at once.

The last few years have been rough for many of us for a plethora of reasons, but I know in my heart of hearts I wouldn't have gotten through it let alone written about it without the incredible support of my near and far-flung community providing flowers and soups and casseroles and heating pads and vent sessions and chocolate covered orange rinds and tote bags and nearly stitch-splitting laughs and a regular reminder that "it's fine, I'm fine, everything's fine" despite not being fine at all. I'm looking at you, Christine, Holly, Alexa, Melissa, Molly, Vanessa, Evelyn, SVT, Bree, Jennie Lew, Amie, Natasha, and Anna.

The Write Minds have made every single poem in this collection, and more, stronger, and I'm indebted to each of them. Thank you, Justin, John, Reagan, Kathleen, Melinda, Cecelia, and Sophie, for encouraging me to reconsider every word, comma, and line break. I'm a better writer because of each of you.

I know I always thank my parents, but golly, I, ironically, don't have enough words to do them justice. I know I've gotten a poem right when I read it to my mother, and she has tears on her cheeks, and just nods at me. Or when my dad, a multi-award-winning novelist, in his notes scribbles "lightning" instead of "lightning bug." I do not believe there has ever been a writer as loved and supported by her parents, unless it is my sister, Caitlin, and boy, are you in for a fascinating read if you pick up any of her work. (You really should. Especially now.)

And while I acknowledge that the acknowledgments are now longer than any poem in the book, I would be utterly remiss not to thank my husband, James. The poems don't even scratch the surface of the greatness of this man's love for me or mine for him. I honestly don't know how I would have survived the last two years without him. He floods our home with joy and hope and silliness and the kind of support we haven't created words for yet. And when I'm so overwhelmed by it all, he reminds me to remember Mr. Rogers and "look for the helpers," of which he is the very best one. I'm so grateful that we have forever ahead of us, because not even death.

Rowe Carenen is a graduate of Salem College and the University of Southern Mississippi. Her poems have appeared in various literary journals and magazines, including the digital eighth issue of *Womanly Mag, The Revenant Culture, GERM, Terrible Orange Review, Oyster River Pages,* and the *Running with Water* anthology. Her first collection, *In the Meantime,* was published by Neverland Publishing in 2014. Unsolicited Press published her best-selling second collection of poetry, *First Drafts from the Brewery*, in April of 2022. She lives in Greenville, SC, with her husband, the Feral Family of Cats, the inside cats (Minerva Jane and Tia Marissa), Sebastian the turtle, and Neville Jameson, their rescue boxer/pittie mix. You can usually find her under her book quilt with a cuppa tea and at least three books in various stages of read.

www.ingramcontent.com/pod-product-compliance
Lightning Source LLC
LaVergne TN
LVHW090540110826
845146LV00003B/1194

* 9 7 9 8 8 9 9 9 0 4 0 1 1 *